W0114646

01 14

Copyright © 2016 by Potter Style, a division of
Penguin Random House LLC

All rights reserved.

Published in the United States by Potter Style, an imprint of
the Crown Publishing Group, a division of Penguin Random
House LLC, New York.

www.crownpublishing.com

www.clarksonpotter.com

POTTER STYLE is a trademark and POTTER STYLE
with colophon is a registered trademark of
Penguin Random House LLC.

ISBN 978-0-553-45962-3

Printed in China

Cover and interior design by Danielle Deschenes

10 9 8 7 6 5 4 3 2 1

First Edition